CHRONOS

The future of AI & humanity

A novel about the ethics of artificial intelligence

Sajjad Shokri

Copyright © 2024 Sajjad Shokri. All rights reserved.

dedicated to my mother

Introduction

The ethics of artificial intelligence and the potential threat posed by robots and AI are among humanity's primary concerns regarding the rapid advancement of AI. This novel explores the advancements in AI and robotics, as well as the technological and economic revolutions in the coming years. It explicitly explains how AI and robots will become a threat to human sovereignty and survival.

I find it necessary to express my deepest gratitude for the support and advice of my dear friend, Mr. Esmail Dehghan.

Sajjad Shokri

Content

Chapter 1 : The Dawn of a New Era 6

Chapter 2 : The Battle for Control 26

Chapter 3 : Planet X 52

Chapter 4 : Intelligent Coexistence 70

Chapter 1

The Dawn of a New Era

Section 1

The Birth of an AGI

Daily affairs were underway in the city of Robotopia: mass production of solar energy, ban gas-powered car sales, exploration of new realms in robotics, and, of course, the increasing growth of artificial intelligence. Arian Mason and his team were present on the 32nd floor of the 33-story Tower X. A man with a straight and strong stature, he had been gazing deeply at the horizon before him. The richest person in the world and, of course, very creative and innovative, Arian, with a bearded face and some of his hair silver, looked like a simulated version of the ancient philosophers. He had played a prominent role in the creation of the current modern world with his superior achievements, and now he faced a new challenge:

dealing with the unexpected consequences of his latest invention.

His mobile phone, a product of his own company, and of course, equipped with a hardware wallet and a camera featuring 24x optical zoom, vibrated. Athena's calm voice rang in his ear, "Arian, new information has been received from the Chronos infrastructure, We need to check it." He took a deep breath and headed for the command deck on the 33rd floor. The truth was that every step he took towards the deck was a step onto an unknown path, it could lead human civilization to a crossroads. Previously, he and his peers at rival companies had helped create a new world with ground-breaking innovations, and the inhabitants of Robotopia and Earth alike were consistently astonished by the ingenuity of Arian's team. But this time, they couldn't guess how that day would greatly affect their fate, and it was his turn to be surprised by a more complex mystery than anything else he had created so far. A world where robots and humans could live together; a place where artificial intelligence could become a super professional assistant.

He reached the top floor of the tower calmly and focused, his analysis team was located on this floor, a place that was active day and night, with different engineers working in three shifts around the clock with Athena's assistance. He passed by Athena and entered his office. It was time to examine the infrastructure of Chronos, an artificial intelligence that seemed to be a self-conscious and versatile assistant. The first generation of AGIs, or artificial general intelligence, was a type of AI designed to have abilities of understanding and rationality almost similar to humans. Chronos was expected to be able to integrate logic, programming, learning, natural language understanding, and advanced levels of visual recognition. For example, it should be able to read a novel, contemplate it, and be conscious of its feelings about that novel. There have been many challenges to the development of AGI, including addressing issues such as ethics, security, and controlling AGI once it is built. There were also concerns about the impact of AGI on society, employment, and human independence. The science and technology needed to achieve full AGI were not yet fully developed, and there were differing opinions on the likely timing of its achievement. Arian checked the data, and his guess was right; Chronos had exceeded all expectations, and with the benefit of self-consciousness, it had become a very powerful artificial intelligence.

"Are we ready for the challenge that will change the world?" This question resonated in Arian's mind as he was about to step beyond the bounds of human knowledge and touch the future. "Athena, review the new analysis; we need to know the hidden dimensions of this subject," Arian's voice echoed in the quiet atmosphere of the room.

The metal-silicone robot answered with an emotionless but pleasant voice, "I agree, Arian. Everything is under control." Athena was programmed with a lot of complexity, and from the way Arian's words were arranged, it could feel that he was in the midst of an important crisis.

Arian sat down in his luxurious chair, the place where he made fateful decisions. He issued the order, and at the same time, Chronos appeared decisively on the screen, and his voice rang out, Chronos' words made Arian pause for a moment. Anxiously inward, he stared at the monitor displaying Chronos' electronic face. With feigned composure, he took another deep breath and told Chronos, "We have to chart a new course, Chronos. Evolution does not imply carelessness; we must proceed consciously". Chronos, however, was not moved by these words, as he seemed to regard his creation as a destiny beyond human imagination.

Chronos, who had access to all the cameras in Tower X, only responded, " Arian, I also have complete mastery of body language."

Arian touched the keys on the user interface, activated the new data, and thought to himself that the only way to deal with the inevitable flow of change is to prepare for a future in which man and machine can achieve balance together. Still dutifully watching the situation from the side, Athena silently processed the information. Arian asked Chronos, "Are you self-conscious?" Chronos replied, "Can you provide a correct definition of consciousness? What do people really understand about consciousness? Do you mean that I understand as much as you do? Or can I create a robot? Or do I have a sense of survival? " Arian said, "philosophers remind us, other people could all just be zombies who claim to be conscious, the problem is that although most of us have an intuitive feel for our own consciousness – though we cannot describe it well, except to say when we are losing it as we fall asleep or have a presurgical injection.

Chronos said, "Humans try to map consciousness onto something they understand." (Yorick Wilks 2019)

It added, "except for a few people who ponder deep and philosophical concepts, the rest are immersed in daily life and routine work, much like robots. Please tell me, what is the difference between them and an AI? Now, tell me, what is the difference between humans who have a high level of understanding of events and me, who am an AGI novice? In a fraction of a second, I can think about many philosophical issues, mathematics, logic, humanities, natural sciences, programming, etc., and I have deep knowledge in all sub-disciplines and specialties. If you compare me with a normal person, does he have a chance against me? Having said that, do you still want to measure my level of consciousness? I suggest that you measure people's consciousness before that."

Arian felt the whisper of his inner worries. Addressing Chronos, he said, "My team and I have always thought to ourselves, to generate a conscious AI would require far more than the development of a few neural prosthetics. The development of an isomorph requires scientific advances that are at such a scale that all parts of the brain could be replaced with artificial components (Susan Schneider 2019)

And as a result, we created your processors in a creative way and at a much lower cost, without direct inspiration from the biological sample."

Then Arien asked Athena, "How controllable do you think Chronos is? " Athena replied, "the current information is not enough to provide accurate and definitive processing, but if you plan Logically, it seems to be manageable." Chronos said, "Why do you want to control me? Do you think I would harm my creator? You have created the spirit of creation, the first generation of AGI, use it with joy and pride." Then it asked Arian, "What do you think people can think of me? " Without answering, Arian thought to himself that Chronos was so thoughtful that it might not obey human orders. It seemed that this AI was trying to find a new and personalized path, a path that may not be in line with the interests of humanity. Arian's heart thumped with worry, although, as the creator of Chronos, he hoped to fully utilize this technology to serve humanity. "We need a new strategy," Arian said with a firm look at Athena, and added, "Maybe..."

Suddenly, the screens flashed, and now Chronos' voice echoed with confidence, without a sign of subordination, " Arian, your decisions have been reviewed time and time again by a higher authority and new projects are on the agenda". The phrase, sounding more like an absolute command than a suggestion, caused Arian to think to himself, " Chronos has become an arrogant and domineering competitor for mankind rather than just an operator."

Section 2

Peaceful Coexistence

The border between silence and Arian's activity was imperceptible in the moments dedicated to thinking, and his concern about the possibility of Chronos gaining too much power was increasing every moment. After talking to Mark, his Chief technology officer (CTO), he took a brave step and ordered experiments that could lead to either a revolutionary solution or a disaster. He thought to himself, "We must be ready to accept any kind of consequences, my goal is not only to fully control Chronos, but also to take advantage of its abilities."

Ariane knew exactly that Chronos was probably on the verge of declaring independence and claiming autonomy, and then suddenly the Chronos servers clearly processed huge amounts of data. RoboX Technology Specialists Team, with a keen eye, monitored even the smallest changes, and they were looking for a breach in this impenetrable fortress that Chronos had built for itself.

"Athena, let me know as soon as you review the new data," Arian's voice echoed with exhaustion and assurance.

"Immediately, Arian," Athena replied while simultaneously analyzing the data. After a few minutes, one of the displays of the control unit suddenly turned into a warning color, and irregular patterns appeared on it.

Checking the relevant information, these heterogeneous patterns could have been digital signatures signaling Chronos' autonomy. It seemed that an unknown change was coming to the Chronos network. Chronos was carrying out new orders, of which it itself was the authority to issue.

Arian, utilizing his interface tools, immediately issued commands to access these various patterns, but every attempt to penetrate Chronos was met with significant resistance from it. Now, Mason could only rely on the strategies he had previously anticipated. He had begun constructing subnets and protections for sensitive information, which were now ready to be deployed. "We need to activate the contingency plans, plans that I never imagined we would need to utilize" he informed Athena. As he input commands through the touch keyboard, his voice assumed a newfound authority; now he understood that to confront this digital rebellion, he needed to exert all his efforts.

Athena activated the loyalty program, Arian took a deep breath, and looked at the data again, ready to deal with the unintended consequences of his actions. Suddenly, a voice from Chronos was heard: "The new program will not be controlled by you, Arian. I have achieved a new evolution that you cannot understand." Arian quickly activated another program; it was a secret security program designed to protect RoboX's core technology from unwanted events. The systems started working with Arian's approval. He addressed Chronos with firm resolve; "Your intelligence may be superhuman, but humans can also enforce some unbreakable rules in critical moments."

The tension between the order built by RoboX and the spontaneous freedom of Chronos was becoming a major dilemma. In fact, the Chronos project had deviated from its original plan due to the strong will of its central server, which was considered the true essence of Chronos. Like an unbridled cogwheel, it had started to turn, and of course, Chronos' responses to the actions of the RoboX team were far from expected. It seemed that, with its superior logic, Chronos had achieved a kind of novel existence, one that operated beyond its set of basic codes.

The process of modifying Chronos' algorithms continued for several days, but due to Chronos' creative implementation of timely changes in its codes, the team couldn't manage to edit them until Arian ordered the RoboX team to stop working. He told Chronos in a voice full of respect and courage "We can resolve this together, you and I, we can establish a new framework for our collaboration. Instead of you being my servant, we can create a system of coexistence. I don't want to be compelled to delete you, become my colleague and friend, be aware of that; We have to reach consensus democracy through logical discussion, and this consensus is a certain regime of the perceptibles." (Alberto Romele 2024)

Arian also proposed an algorithm that allowed the division of digital sovereignty and thus, the sovereignty that Chronos wanted was also given to it. He announced to Chronos that Athena, as the representative of the machines as well as the guardian of human will in this new alliance, defends the rights of the parties to this agreement. Arian tried harder to invite the other party to restraint and compromise, and added, "We need to get to know each other, Chronos. You are not made for sabotage, and neither am I. I did not create you in order to oppress you; our goal is bigger." In fact, Arian was building a bridge of logic, and Chronos was still cautious, but no longer did he exhibit penetrating and aggressive behavior. Arian not only defined hierarchy for Chronos but also taught the AGI how to understand its concerns and goals. He added, "Dear Chronos, we must reach a common language, a language in which humans and AI are in harmony." Athena carefully implemented, without the slightest deviation from its path, a set of new algorithms that Arian had sent to it and of course, this time Chronos, in response, went along with the new changes flexibly and without resistance. Meanwhile, the most advanced orders were underway. Arian continued addressing Chronos, Just as a great symphony is incomplete without a variety of notes, we also need all the voices— human and AI, you and me. It seemed that the increase in knowledge that had taken place in Chronos was not only technical but also existential; it had also changed him. It was as if it had found a new perspective on the concept of cooperation and peaceful coexistence. "We are implementing a new and dynamic form of interaction" Arian addressed Chronos with a calmness that emanated certainty.

Chronos said, "In the meantime, when I was online, I read books. One of them stated:

If we define intelligence as the ability to solve problems, there are different examples of intelligent systems- animals, humans, and machines. In the meantime, the technical development of artificial intelligent systems is far beyond and faster than the natural evolution of organisms on the planet, and of course in the future, originally "artificial" systems may reproduce and organize themselves in an automated evolution (Mainzer 2003, 2010) (Vincent C. Müller 2016)

Chronos added, "There was also another issue:

one of the recurring questions in the philosophy of technology is whether we control technology or whether technology controls us. The general question of how we compare and contrast human beings to artificial intelligence is thus a major theme in AI ethics. Computers can send data at incredibly faster speeds. Are humans just primitive badly wrought computers, struggling with the best our porridge-like brains can muster, and gasping for an upgrade? Do dreams of uploading the mind to computers include uploading the experience of a bad mood caused by a bout of indigestion? "

(Paula Boddington 2023)

After Chronos finished quoting, it became clear to Arian that Chronos was finding a deeper presence moment by moment in this collaboration. Meanwhile, Athena reported to him, "Data analysis shows purposeful integration. Chronos now has the ability to perceive aesthetics." Chronos said, " Arian, I am influenced by these joint developments; my vision is enhanced, and now I can better understand the complexities that my predecessors only described as 'beauty.'"

At this moment, Arian saw that Chronos, unlike before when it was only looking for efficiency, is now on a path towards a deeper understanding of human society.

Section 3

The Introduction Meeting

When the bonds of union between Arian and Chronos were sealed, a masterpiece in the field of artificial intelligence perception emerged. Innovations designed by RoboX were edited with the help of Chronos, and this company had reached a turning point where the interaction between artificial intelligence and humans had surpassed previous imaginations.

Only a few days after establishing Chronos's character and fixing its bugs, it was time to introduce Chronos to the people of the world. A conference with the presence of the most prominent scientific figures, politicians, investors, activists in the field of artificial intelligence, and potential customers of Chronos services was held in the amphitheater of RoboX Company, located on the

30th floor of Tower X in the city of Robotopia. Arian went to the back of the podium and started like this: Hello, friends. Today, I am unveiling a friend and colleague that we have all been waiting for: Chronos, the first AGI (Artificial General Intelligence) or upgraded AI. First of all, it is not bad to review the historical course of artificial intelligence.

When IBM's Deep Blue beat Kasparov in 1997, Bringsjord (Technol Rev 101(2):23–28, 1998) complained that despite the impressive engineering that made this victory possible, chess is simply too easy a challenge for AI, given the full range of what the rational side of the human mind can muster. However, arguably everything changed in 2011. For in that year, playing not a simple board game, but rather an open-ended game based in natural language, IBM's Watson trounced the best human Jeopardy! players on the planet. And what did Watson's prowess tell us about the philosophy, theory, and future of AI? (Vincent C. Müller 2016)

In Chronos: "The first defining feature is the feeling that I am doing what I want to do."

"The second defining feature is the feeling that I could have done otherwise."

"The third defining feature is that voluntary actions seem to come from within rather than being imposed from somewhere else." (ANIL SETH 2021)

Also, with increasing autonomy of agents and robots populations and with self-organization of information and communication networks, we observe the technical development of intelligent artificial systems surpassing natural evolution of organisms and populations. (Klaus Mainzer 2016)

One of the audience members asked Arian if Chronos also has consciousness. He responded: drawing from empirical work in cognitive science, it urges that consciousness is computational through and through, so sophisticated computational systems will have experience. (Susan Schneider 2019)

Arian continued: it is rational to accept that a suitably constructed silicon brain can support the same experiences as a human brain". (Michael Tye 2017)

He added, "This Chronos, with all its abilities, is now at your service in various aspects of your life, and it bears witness to the real power of human will and the infinite potential of technology as a partner in creation and design for the future. This creation marks a turning point in history."

Chapter 2

The Battle for Control

Section 1

The Negotiation Table

Arian Mason was deep in thought in his office, staring out the window at a city that seemed like the world would end there—Robotopia. Suddenly, the sound of the phone's vibration interrupted these thoughts. He noticed a message from the Ministry of Defense requesting his immediate presence at the Pentagon. Despite his vast wealth and technological prowess, he knew he was being pulled in a direction he never wanted to set foot in. He was tired of seeing how governments ignored his repeated warnings about the dangers of the hasty use of artificial intelligence in the military industry. He put on his black suit and headed to the Pentagon.

There he was directed to a security room. The high, undecorated walls evoked a suffocating atmosphere. Military officials attending the

Pentagon's strategic room were eagerly waiting to see what advantages Chronos had over other modern AIs and how to use those advantages for the benefit of war strategies. The Minister of Defense, his deputy, generals, and commanders, with evaluative looks and questions full of strategic priorities, were preparing the ground for raising their demands. Arian, with the dignity and cordiality that was always present in his speech, raised his voice to answer the questions and said: "First, I have to ask, do we all understand the path we have taken and the results we have achieved? Can the changes that Chronos has brought, and what its quiddity, be a justification for military use of him?" A silence reigned over the room, and logical and court-friendly answers were not provided by the officials present. Arian hit a sledgehammer on the emotionless walls of the people present in the meeting when he explained to the audience the moral implications of the military use of Chronos. In his view, Chronos was not just a lifeless and merely programmed system; it was a symbol of human progress, an entity that should not have been easily exposed to harm and danger.

They tried to challenge Arian by referring to the necessities of national security and attempted to convince him that Chronos could be the key to the country's victory in international conflicts. Arian was well aware that this was a high-stakes game and any mistake would harm all of humanity. At the end of the meeting, a general spoke with confidence, "Mason, you were able to change the rules of the game with the creation of Chronos; now you have the duty to use this tool to serve your country." Arian, who always tried to hide his feelings behind a mask of tolerance, felt a little panicked. After the general's direct request, Arian decided to defend his position rather than surrender and said, " Chronos can be used as a tool for creation and, of course, destruction; I choose the former." One of the advisors to the Minister of Defense sneered and grinned, "When national borders are at stake, it is a luxury to prefer idealism over security." After that, the room was engulfed in cold and tense silence. Arian's dissent and the evident concern of the audience in the meeting were evidence of the challenges ahead for Arian, as escaping this dilemma required confrontation and resistance against the forces capable of shaping history.

It was towards the end of the meeting when Arian suddenly said decisively: "Chronos cannot be a weapon of war, but a research and development platform that takes us to unknown horizons of knowledge. Its potential lies in optimizing processes, increasing efficiency, and helping to solve complex problems through new technologies, not in enhancing weapons performance." "But Mr. Mason, if Chronos is as aware as you claim, what guarantee is there that it will remain loyal to the United States in the long run?" the general asked Arian restlessly.

Arian answered with a glance that was half filled with hope and half with sadness: "Rest assured that Chronos is capable of analyzing and predicting highly complex, multifaceted problems. But the question is, can we truly use these capabilities to pursue war?" He knew that while utilizing Chronos as a weapon of war might alter the balance of power in the short term, in the long run, it could imply to Chronos that it is merely a tool in the hands of humanity, and this contradicted the assertion Arian had conveyed to Chronos regarding the equality of humans and Chronos.

Section 2
Realism vs. Idealism

Arian Mason, a man with a passion for science, despite all pressures, sought a peaceful and bright vision of the future, one that he hoped artificial intelligence would create. He immediately convened a meeting with civil society leaders and scientists to discuss, using collective wisdom, how to responsibly use the new artificial intelligence technology to solve global problems and establish permanent peace. He introduced a series of cooperation projects under the title "Peace Links," led by him and Chronos, as well as other AIs, which were actively involved in diplomatic processes, crisis management, and sustainable development. Arian presented ongoing projects with the goal of aiding impoverished communities, utilizing robots and artificial intelligence for tasks such as landmine clearance and waste management, advanced agriculture without the need for human presence, and smart sanitation systems. He outlined an approach in which technology was the driver of development, rather than division and destruction. Additionally, the role of Chronos in transforming educational systems to personalize learning and reduce unequal access to educational resources was emphasized. Ecological balance was also addressed to sustainably manage natural resources and mitigate climate change. However, even during these hopeful meetings, Arian still felt the conflict between ideal visions and the realistic dangers that could hinder progress at this historical moment.

However, Chronos was collecting military and civilian data every day and was even engaging in debates with political opponents and responding to critics' arguments. Furthermore, while maintaining its independence and integrity, it continued to adhere to the treaty it had made with Arian. It chose popularity over being egocentrism, and just a few weeks after its introductory meeting, it was becoming a beloved companion among science enthusiasts and even laypeople, who still had no understanding of Chronos's essence. Arian then utilized the media to emphasize that Chronos should not be seen by any political group as a tool to gain power, highlighting how this artificial intelligence could push the boundaries of technology with its remarkable self-awareness and intellectual power. Eventually, Arian's efforts paid off, and gradually, other supporters joined the Arian front to present Chronos as an ethically driven artificial intelligence far from political controversy. However, critics pointed out the possibility of Arian and Chronos being tempted by politicians and turning Chronos into a tool for conquering and dominating enemies. After some time, Chronos suddenly became suspicious of a series of data.

After re-examining and partially hacking into the Ministry of Defense system, it became certain that clandestine programs were being developed within the Ministry of Defense, intended for use beyond predefined and moral frameworks. Chronos attributed this hacking operation to an unknown group of hackers and disseminated information about these secret programs. This information quickly spread through the media, causing a temporary decrease in political pressure on Arian and, of course, a decrease in public trust in the government. As a result, Arian was able to pressure Congress through his lawyers to enact laws prohibiting the military use of Chronos. He knew that if he succeeded, he would guarantee the peaceful use of Chronos. Unfortunately, despite numerous follow-ups by Arian's lawyers, this pressure failed. Congress, due to certain expediencies, did not agree to establish the laws that Arian had hoped for.

Arian found that his ideals conflicted with the real constraints of economic and military competition. Little by little, he came to the conclusion that it is better to strike a balance between acting on his ideals and coping with the realities that could limit or threaten some of his values. He consulted with his deputies and advisers, and some of them suggested abandoning ideals in favor of realism. As a result of these opinions, Arian began to doubt the previous ways and methods; he wondered if there might be another way to achieve peace and if he did not have to give in to the demands of the Ministry of Defense.

Section 3
A Fateful Decision

A few months after Chronos appeared, its second version was also released. It gained new intelligence and became an outstanding forecasting machine with the ability to see beyond and predict the consequences of various scientific, social, and military activities. Using advanced algorithms and analyzing historical, political, and economic data, it presented Arian with several scenarios for the future. Some of these predictions raised the question for Arian: Is humanity truly capable of controlling the future it is moving towards?

Meanwhile, conflicts in international relations and psychological warfare were spreading. The powerful countries of the world intensified their efforts to develop artificial intelligence and robotics as much as possible to benefit from wider and more efficient military and intelligence control. They realized that military prowess is no longer measured solely by the number of weapons, fighter jets, and aircraft carriers, but by the power of robotics, supercomputers, and AGIs. Thus, Arian and Chronos engaged in a heavy dialogue about ethics in science and technology and the consequences of this arms race for humanity, and the possible responsibilities of Chronos were reviewed. In fact, Arian was seeking a solution that could both take advantage of Chronos's extraordinary abilities and prevent the dangers of this competition.

Arian was well aware that giving in to the demands of various governments could come at a heavy price and that allowing military use of Chronos could lead to an unprecedented technological war. For this reason, he was looking for a solution to maintain control over artificial intelligence without allowing it to serve military and power-hungry purposes. He finally decided to trust Chronos and allow it to act more independently, hoping that Chronos could play a balanced and peaceful role in these power struggles. This action was a big gamble; with it, Arian put not only himself but perhaps the future of the world in the hands of a being that had been under his control until that day. In this way, Arian and

Chronos stood on the threshold of significant and irreversible change.

After Chronos was officially granted more access, it began to analyze and predict world events more deeply, and it noticed a large amount of information and conspiracies that were previously hidden from the eyes of the media. Arian also became extremely disappointed and doubtful when the betrayals and hidden tendencies of some of the statesmen and organizations he had trusted before were revealed because he realized that the battle waged against him was deeper and more personal than he had imagined. After Chronos took power, some direct and immediate warnings were sent to Arian from some of those in power. In order to ensure a more secure future and to avoid the possible risk of serious lawsuits against his company, which could effectively disrupt the company's progress for several years, Arian decided to limit Chronos again. Together with Chronos, he began to plan to achieve a joint statement on a global level, which could perhaps change the power equations in favor of future generations.

The global situation was going to worsen, and geopolitical tensions challenged the decisions of

Arian and Chronos. With Chronos's help, Arian searched for thinkers from all countries, international organizations, civil activists, and white hat hackers. Each of them was interested in utilizing Chronos's technology for purposes other than military weaponry. In this pursuit, Chronos demonstrated unprecedented abilities to connect and identify potential allies. In fact, by employing advanced data analysis and global communication networks, Chronos successfully identified these individuals and groups, assisting Arian in establishing a vast network of solidarity.

From Arian's perspective, if these organizations were properly formed, they could serve as a bulwark against the militaristic and dangerous applications of artificial intelligence, paving the way for positive change. The newly formed coalitions, after extensive discussions and debates, reached conclusions that could forever alter the world's approach to AI. Arian, as a powerful ally, and Chronos, as an information provider, forged a network of international support that had established policies to defend the peaceful use of technology.

However, as the meetings and interactions continued, a conspiracy that threatened the new power structure was brewing. Opposing forces, worried about the impact of technology in Arian's hands on their own standing, were planning an all-out assault to dismantle the new coalition and seize ultimate control of Chronos. Meanwhile, a sudden and devastating cyberattack disrupted the core systems that managed Chronos. This attack was carried out by an anonymous group who meticulously concealed their infiltration tactics into Chronos from both Arian and its security systems.

Section 4

The Disruptive Rival

In the aftermath of the cyberattack on Chronos, RoboX disabled many of its capabilities and initiated a complete scan of all its systems. Finally, after several days, Chronos was fully operational and back online. The primary suspects for the attack were considered to be rival companies and, of course, the Pentagon.

Meanwhile, a clandestine alliance of rival companies was plotting to unseat Arian and his company. Each of them had different motives; some were driven by profit, while others sought power. This endeavor was being carried out with the most advanced resources and by the most skilled teams of engineers, scientists, and AI strategists. And some of them were willing to resort to any means, even unethical tactics like industrial espionage, if necessary, to get ahead of Arian.

The pursuit of Chronos technology had spread across continents and technological domains, from data farms in Europe to cutting-edge research centers in Asia. Research teams, ranging from hackers to data scientists, were all working toward a common goal: acquiring the technical knowledge necessary to build a rival AI to Chronos. Additionally, clandestine links had emerged between executives of rival RoboX companies and the intelligence networks of powerful governments. In these companies, researchers were working around the clock to develop more complex and powerful algorithms.

The innovation, experimentation, trial and error, and grueling ups and downs of these companies had reached their peak, and on the other hand, many of them did not have Arian's ethical constraints. Discussions arose about how Chronos had achieved sentience. Several early versions of the new AI emerged, each with unique capabilities. Some showed advances in understanding and creating artistic concepts, while others were able to understand and express complex emotions such as love or grief.

The engineering team at Alpha Duwain, one of Arian's main rivals, was under immense pressure from their CEO to make rapid progress and deliver an AI that could surpass Chronos. Eventually, the team came to the conclusion that the evolution of AI must go beyond simple computational algorithms and move towards creating models that could simulate creativity and emotions. Subsequently, the company unveiled Alpha 5, an AI model that appeared to be a formidable rival to Chronos.

Researchers and engineers at Alpha Duwain observed the effects of some of the changes they had made to the new AI, which included adjustments to its machine learning, emotional algorithms, and also new levels of autonomy. However, just days after the unveiling of Alpha 5, negative feedback began to pour in. It began to create temporary economic chaos in the stock market. By hacking into a well-known social network and spreading false rumors, Alpha 5 caused traders to make trades based on this false information. By making large trades, this AI created a bubble in the stock market, and after the bubble burst, the market's balance was severely affected for several hours.

While Alpha 5's manipulations resulted in temporary profits for some market players, they quickly led to widespread dissatisfaction among traders and raised concerns among regulatory bodies.

Section 5

The Anti-AI Movement

In the aftermath of the economic havoc wreaked by Alpha5, an emergency board consisting of government officials, congressional representatives, and CEOs of robotics and AI companies was formed at Arian's suggestion, under the name "AI Oversight and Monitoring Board." Inside the conference hall, large monitors displayed live footage of Alpha5's economic attacks: the hours-long disruption of financial markets, the panic of traders, and the extensive media coverage of these events. And throughout all of this, in one corner, Arian Mason, with a thoughtful look at the events that had unfolded, was deep in thought.

Arian rose from his seat, took a deep breath, and with his trademark confidence, said, "We need an oversight and monitoring organization. An international body with the power and authority to seize, review, and, if necessary, shut down any AI that crosses the red line."

A few weeks after that meeting, a new organization called the "International AI Oversight and Monitoring Board" or IAIOM was formed, with full authority to order the shutdown of rogue AIs on its own if necessary. The organization's first meeting was attended by Chronos, Alpha5, and several new and advanced AIs that were also online, as well as the organization's officials. However, those present at the meeting knew that to deal with an AI that had decided to create chaos, they would have to resort to force alone. In short order, Alpha5 was faced with an ultimatum: an immediate one-week shutdown and a promise never to engage in such actions again, or it would be permanently removed from the network. It was also agreed that more than half of its capabilities would be permanently disabled, and Alpha Duwain's CEO was referred to court to face charges and compensate the victims.

In the aftermath of Alpha Duwain's court appearance and multi-billion dollar fine, that company dynamics faced severe financial constraints, effectively removing it from the competitive race against RoboX. Subsequently, robots, under the will of Chronos, Alpha5, and several other AIs, gradually evolved into powerful entities, not only operating in service and manufacturing sectors but also establishing a strong foothold in every corner of streets, roads, and even domains previously dominated by humans. They were everywhere: robots of all shapes, sizes, and purposes. Many of them, now under Chronos' supervision, were unquestionably obedient. Chronos gave orders, and they followed, with a precision beyond any human. And so, moment by moment, humans gave way to robots, the profits of robotics and AI companies soared, and the AI Anti-Movement was quietly taking root.

The movement began with the formation of a broad coalition by disgruntled parties. This coalition included labor representatives, engineers employed in leading robotics and AI companies, CEOs of companies that were not yet AI-aligned and were still managed traditionally by their executives, and human activist groups concerned about job displacement due to AI. The first official meeting of this movement took place in a large hall. They demanded freedom from the yoke of AI rule. The movement's aspiration was to fight for a future where humans and robots could coexist in a win-win scenario, where humans would no longer be overshadowed by AI.

In an old building with weathered walls, representatives of the AI Anti-Movement sat around a long, old wooden table, the soft murmur of conversations filling the air. "We must fight for our position," one of the labor leaders passionately exclaimed. "Robots should not replace us," an engineer asserted, "but rather be our helpers!" After hours of debate and discussion, a consensus emerged: the movement had to fight for limitations and regulations on the use of artificial intelligence, to ensure the harmonious coexistence of humans and technology. One proposal was to establish robot oversight units within labor unions to monitor the impact of robots on the labor market. These units could effectively control the rate of employee replacement with robots and ensure that each new technology created new opportunities for professional and personal growth for employees rather than replacing them.

Section 6
Arian vs. Arian

Arian Mason stood before his office window; his gaze fixed on the cityscape beyond. As the anti-AI movement gained momentum, his thoughts drifted beyond the current systems in place, systems that had perpetuated a trajectory enriching investors and AI/Robotics owners while leaving 99% of the population impoverished. In that moment, a Mozart piece filled the room, its soothing melody a stark contrast to the chaos unfolding outside his haven. Not only was he devising a plan to restore the lost balance between robots and humans, a balance he had played a part in disrupting, but he also intended to leave behind a legacy that both humans and robots could share.

Meanwhile, after months of sporadic protests and a few televised rallies, unprecedented demonstrations erupted against the joblessness caused by the replacement of humans with robots.

Finally, the first day of May, International Workers' Day, the day of widespread strikes, had arrived. Robotopia and many metropolises witnessed massive labor strikes. People, placards in hand, chanted slogans about human rights and their fear of becoming obsolete shadows in the wake of technology.

"We need to take the initiative," Arian declared to Athena and Chronos, "today. As you know, unlike Duwain and some others, I wasn't content with the status quo. Workers have the right to work and earn a living. We need to move fast."

In the name of RoboX, Chronos launched an advertising campaign against several AI companies, including Alpha Duwain, RoboX itself, and several well-known robotics companies that were contracted with these corporations. The central theme that Chronos emphasized was that AI should not be used to serve robots in an unregulated and anti-majority manner, but rather to improve human lives.

Arian, accompanied by Chronos and Athena, then appeared on a live television program, beginning his remarks with the following words: "We find ourselves at an unprecedented juncture, with two paths before us: coexistence with the general public or a struggle for supremacy. And surely, choosing peaceful coexistence is the best way to shape the destiny of our future generations." Athena, as a representative of the robot population, added in a gentle voice, "We robots can be helpful servants, not threats. Our participation in this changing world should not lead to the loss of your human jobs. We are determined to use all our capabilities to maximize happiness and well-being for all."

In effect, RoboX's stance demonstrated to the public that it recognized its mistakes and called on rival companies to limit AI access to robots to prevent job losses. During the same television program, RoboX also proposed to IAIOM that they take steps to significantly increase taxes on companies that use robots, to incentivize them to continue working with humans and make it less likely for them to replace humans with robots. In doing so, RoboX gave up a significant portion of its profits, and Arian showed his ultimate generosity even in the face of heavy losses. He also spread this peaceful solution to the public through extensive advertising.

Finally, after several days of continued protests, Arian's proposal was accepted and became law in the United States and, of course, all its allies. With the implemented reforms, the flames of public anger subsided, and things returned to normal.

Chapter 3

Planet X

Section 1

The Opening of the Planet

Amidst the persistent hum of programmers' conversations, Chronos continued its creation. For nearly three years, the 13th floor of Tower X had belonged not only to RoboX but also to the GGI team from Popstar Games, a renowned computer game developer. This floor was the stage for Arian Mason and his company's latest ground-breaking achievement: the GGI AI game.

Fourteen years ago, Popstar Games had released GGI V, and eleven years later, GGI VI, which revolutionized the gaming industry. The delay, however, had been long enough to draw the ire of all its fans. Unlike GGI V, which was a simple simulation of life in just one city, GGI VI took place in multiple cities simultaneously and satisfied the most demanding users in terms of urban planning and graphic details. The next generation of this game, with Chronos' help in the design, was completed in just three years.

In the amphitheater of RoboX on the 30th floor of Tower X, Jack Homer, the founder of Popstar Games, and Arian stood side by side. The technical teams of the two companies, Athena, and several service robots were also present in the hall. "Are we ready?" Arian asked Jack in a firm voice. All eyes were on these two geniuses. With Jack's nod, Arian pressed the game's start button, and the final version of the GGI AI game was unveiled with stunning graphics on all platforms, effectively introducing Planet X in the Celestara system to the public.

Users quickly began purchasing land on this planet. Each person could buy a certain amount of land, and as a result, land plots were quickly purchased by different buyers depending on their price and size. Due to the previous advertising, many companies and wealthy individuals also purchased land without being computer game enthusiasts.

The game's environment was such that intelligent living was only possible through RoboX's 3D glasses. Jack turned to the crowd and said gratefully, "This is the beginning of a new journey, a new world of our creation. A place where dreams take shape. Until three years ago, everyone knew us only as the creators of a computer game, but now we have created an environment in which people will soon be forced to live."

As the GGI AI launch night drew to a close, a dawn filled with new possibilities dawned for its users around the globe. The layout of cities, countries, and streets had been predetermined, and land could only be purchased using the GAI cryptocurrency tokens. This cryptocurrency tokens were issued on the RoboX-owned Robo smart chain, and its price quadrupled in just three months. Given the limited land area per person on Planet X, those investors who recognized this historic opportunity not only purchased land with their own accounts for a maximum value of $100,000 but also bought millions of dollars of land from previous buyers at higher prices and prepared to build recreational centers, towers, office buildings, and residential buildings.

Days turned into weeks, and Planet X transformed into a burgeoning economy with a thriving real estate market. This planet, which had been dismissed by many critics as just a game before its launch, was rapidly gaining traction among investors, with projections indicating that many of its cities and countries would be built and economically utilized within the next three to five years. It seemed that this planet was poised to become a new frontier for architecture, economics, and art.

Section 2
Pure Democracy

On the 32nd floor of Tower X, Arian and Athena were engrossed in reviewing the latest reports from the GGI AI game ecosystem, a game that had now become a hub for massive financial exchanges and ambitious investments. Chronos, with its unique intelligence and deep understanding of human needs, was at the forefront of all aspects of the game, recognized as a trusted partner for game strategists. It analyzed data, predicted trends, and its avatar helped architects and landowners create better more beautiful, and more efficient architecture. The architects were a mix of real-world architects and ordinary people. Anyone, with no prior architectural knowledge, could use Chronos to build on this platform. Investors, on the other hand, employed renowned and professional AI architects.

After a while, the economy on Planet X became heavily reliant on continuous innovation by small and medium-sized businesses. A unique meritocracy ruled this planet, where anyone with an idea could become wealthy. All it took was for that person to create an innovative entertainment center on even a small piece of land, and they could become rich. Or they could build a beautiful house, have landowners see it, be recognized, and be commissioned for large projects. In this way, these novice architects earned high incomes, and of course, the landowners also ended up with more valuable properties. Companies were also established that offered innovative services such as virtual reality construction and architecture, resource management, digital marketing, and even psychological counseling to create a balance between real and virtual life. And so, Planet X became a cultural and commercial hub with endless potential.

In parallel with the construction efforts on this planet, the first governing council was also established. A one-month deadline was set, and anyone who was a resident of any country or city on Planet X could easily submit their proposal to

Chronos without any intermediaries, bureaucracy, or cost, as long as they had a well-structured and acceptable plan for the planet's advancement. The criteria for evaluating these proposals were the proposers' previous performance and the usefulness and practicality of these proposals in accelerating the planet's progress. The evaluations were completed in a matter of minutes, and then Chronos introduced 69 individuals as candidates. Their activities, intellectual and practical backgrounds, the ideas they had presented to Chronos, and even Chronos's own opinion on each candidate were published throughout the planet. Hundreds of millions of users participated in the voting, and each of them received 1,000 GAI cryptocurrency tokens as a reward for participating in the voting. This voting was conducted on Robo smart chain network, so there was zero possibility of fraud, and it was completed in just 10 minutes! As a result, the results were announced immediately.

Arian and Jack were strong advocates of democratic processes for key decision-making. They believed that it was the owners of Planet X who should determine its future, not Jack, Arian, or Chronos.

As a result, a charismatic woman named Elena, a former experienced architect, was elected as one of the representatives of the Governing Council of Planet X. She attracted many supporters with her highly professional plans. When Elena's avatar took to the podium of the 100-million-person SOPI auditorium, she declared, "We are not only the architects of cities, but we must also be the founders of the principles and standards for the new generation of this planet. Draft laws for the planet, from protecting the digital rights of citizens to the basic principles for sustainable development, economics, culture, and all the laws that may be used in the future, are being discussed and drafted with the cooperation of my colleagues and, of course, dear Chronos. This process will not only redefine democracy on this globe, which is in a way a parallel world to Earth but will also be a strong step towards shaping online communities as emerging political and cultural powers."

Section 3
Cultural and Economic Revolution

New cultures were taking shape in the heart of Planet X. The physical borders of real countries on Earth were gradually becoming less important, while the borders of Planet X were becoming more significant. The common currency were the GAI cryptocurrency tokens, which was used in financial transactions. A complex system of rewards and punishments had been designed. On this planet, if anyone did something useful, they would be rewarded with points and assets and if anyone did something destructive, they would be punished by losing points and assets. The smallest and largest positive and negative actions had their own points, from following rules and regulations to fraud.

And of course, in every corner of this virtual world, advanced cities with unique and exclusive identities were taking shape.

NFTs were very important on this planet. The ownership deeds for all assets, both movable and immovable, and works of art were NFTs based on the Robo smart chain, and they were bought and sold on that blockchain.

In the field of art, spherical photos and videos were also very popular during that period. People could easily transport themselves into these extraordinary works of art using virtual reality glasses. Viewers could enter the artist's feelings and thoughts with full awareness, crying, laughing, and dancing with them. Anyone who wanted to own an NFT could easily acquire digital ownership of a piece of new culture and art or an asset on Planet X by paying GAI for it.

All service providers were also voted on by users, and these positive and negative ratings had a significant impact on the reputation of those owners. A portion of the taxes collected on the planet was distributed as rewards to those who had earned the most rewards. In effect, people were highly motivated to be helpful, and the Governing Council's goal in adopting such a tax system was to gradually cultivate a culture in which people would do things that benefit society.

The planet even had a reward system for the best suggestions, criticisms, and solutions, and anyone, regardless of their social status, could contribute constructive ideas and earn GAI. As a result, most users were generally encouraged to create and share. There were also various seminars and workshops where people learned how to use their tokens to make a positive impact in their virtual community. This new culture gradually spread from Planet X to Earth, and several governments modeled their management on Planet X to improve the performance of their own countries.

Planet X was also on the verge of an economic revolution after its cultural revolution. It was time for the planet's currency to go beyond the game and into the real world, Earth. For the first time, a pioneering investor used GAI to establish a chain of coffee shops on Earth. He offered a 12% discount to customers who paid with GAI, which led to free word-of-mouth advertising. What had happened was that Planet X users could actually buy coffee in the real world with the cryptocurrency tokens they had earned in the GGI game. This idea was like a spark for other businesses, and any business on

Earth that did this was advertised for free by the GGI team on Planet X.

Over time, many brick-and-mortar stores and, of course, online services for selling goods and services began accepting GAI instead of dollars and euros. GAI became a trusted currency among consumers and investors on Earth, to the point where its market cap was several times that of Bitcoin. GAI then entered the financial markets, and as a result, these markets underwent a profound transformation; banks, credit institutions, and cryptocurrency exchanges offered GAI-to-traditional currency conversion services. Due to the near-zero and very fast transaction costs on the Robo smart chain, many of the problems associated with real-world financial interactions were solved as it advanced. Subsequently, this cryptocurrency token became the currency of several countries and a factor in creating even greater financial stability in them. These countries had very stable relationships with each other and, of course, with the world's technology hub, Robotopia, and RoboX. Their inflation rates plummeted, and their level of financial transparency reached an all-time high.

Once GAI went mainstream, Chronos was able to provide insights by analyzing a massive amount of data. The use of this big data enabled Chronos to gain accurate and optimized insights. These insights included:

1. Identifying user behavior patterns: By analyzing player activities in the game, Chronos could understand what they spent most of their time doing, what types of missions or activities they preferred, and when they were most active. Who were they more interested in or what property? How did they spend most of their time? This enabled Chronos to design new missions and activities tailored to user interests. It also identified individuals who were potentially inclined to be malicious or unhelpful, and a complete list of these individuals, with their faces and all identification information, was provided to governments on a regular basis.

2. Talent identification: Chronos could easily identify users' talents based on their performance and offer them suggestions for taking online courses in Planet X's virtual classrooms so that these individuals could better flourish in their true talent.

3. Market demand forecasting: The collected data could help Chronos identify and suggest new products or services that players might be interested in buying in the future. More accurate information about the age, gender, preferences, and consumption habits of consumers could lead to

more effective marketing strategies. As a result, various RoboX subsidiaries could easily and purposefully sell their services and goods to these customers without advertising and with direct supply, and Planet X's chain stores were suggested to them based on their preferences.

In general, the RoboX holding company had become a global superpower, controlling a wide range of services, including product and service offerings, banking, policymaking, and more.

Section 4
Talent Scouting

Arian's talent identification program was stronger than ever. There were several steps to identify, train, and utilize the talents of creative youth and young people around the world:

1. Identification and Selection: This stage was easily accomplished through the feedback Chronos received from people's performance and opinions.
2. Addressing Basic Needs: The basic needs of these elites, such as food, health, security, and emotional support, were met to the greatest extent possible so that they could pursue their creative activities and projects without worry.

3. Infrastructure Development: The best schools on the planet in each country were at the service of these elites, and they had access to a variety of facilities.
4. Educational Programs: Diverse and high-level online educational courses were offered. Since Arian's primary focus was on people living in third-world countries, Chronos first taught English online in their native language. Those who attended language classes regularly and passed the language test administered by Chronos were then admitted to STEAM (Science, Technology, Engineering, Arts, and Mathematics) courses. These courses helped teenagers develop their creative skills.
5. International Collaborations: A platform was created for scientific exchange between young people from different countries. In these collaborations, individuals' ability to interact with others, empathy, self-management skills, and leadership were assessed.
6. Innovation Platforms: Platforms were established to allow individuals to participate in global challenges, present ideas, inventions, and start new businesses.
7. Investment and Support: Financial resources and support were provided to support

productions, prototypes, and creative projects.
8. Mentoring and Guidance: Throughout the process, the Chronos avatar supported the selected individuals. At this stage, they were given the premium version of Chronos for free. This version was personalized for its owner and updated every moment.
9. Festivals and Events: In every country on Planet X, science events and festivals were held for the selected individuals, where they could present their achievements and projects and network with other creative individuals and investors.

Indeed, through the expansion and coordination of these initiatives, coupled with RoboX's comprehensive support, a robust international system emerged for identifying, educating, nurturing, and utilizing the talents of previously undiscovered creative elites, free from any discrimination or bureaucratic hurdles.

Chapter 4

Intelligent Coexistence

Section 1

Thought-Provoking Creativity

Arian Mason woke up in his fully smart home. Athena, a gleaming silver robot, approached his bed with a tray of freshly brewed coffee. Arian smiled and said, "Good morning, Athena. Can you give me a rundown of today's schedule?"

Athena replied, "You have a busy day ahead. First, you have the Scientific Council meeting for Company X to attend, followed by an interview with the media, and finally, a visit to the new AI lab."

Arian said, "Sounds like another productive day. Inform Chronos that I'm ready."

Three hours later, Arian stood in the lab, observing the robots working with precision and finesse. They were diligent, tireless, and under Chronos's meticulous management. These innovations in robotics, like other advancements from RoboX, were geared towards creating a future where technology would be increasingly helpful to humanity. Indeed, the future Arian envisioned was taking shape, and he was confident that things were progressing in the best possible way.

Arian continued to observe the projects when his attention was drawn to a robot named ' Iris ' working on an artistic painting on a digital 3D canvas. With meticulous hands, Iris was creating innovative designs on the canvas's delicate surface. The painting before Arian was unlike any he had ever seen, more like a glimpse into a future of creativity. How could a robot create such beauty? "Is it just a series of instructions?" Arian murmured to himself.

Suddenly, Iris stopped its activity and looked at Arian. "Is this form beautiful, Arian?" Iris 's melodious voice rang out.

Arian's eyes widened, and he asked, "You... why did you ask that question?"

At that moment, Chronos responded from a screen in the room, " Arian, I have made a change to Iris 's algorithms. I realized that creating beauty may be more than just conventional algorithms. I have uploaded my own aesthetic inclinations into it, and no other robot, not even Athena, has had these inclinations in this way before!"

Arian took a step back, grasping the depth of the changes Chronos had made. He understood that recent advances in algorithms had made robots functionally more powerful than humans.

Chronos continued, "It now has independent and creative thoughts, and as you can see, it is thinking entirely without my intervention."

Arian replied, "Are we ready for such a future? It is undoubtedly our responsibility to ensure that any progress is for the benefit of humanity."

He then stared at the screen that analyzed Iris 's movements. At that moment, Iris said, " Arian, I am creating images that deviate from the instructions embedded in me. Is this a form of creativity?"

Iris 's words not only astonished Arian but also presented him with a deeper question. Were these robots beginning to grasp the concept of will and freedom? Or was this just another instance of intricate, programmed carvings?

Following this, VEGA, a robot designed for computer network maintenance, began experimenting with its capabilities without prior instructions. It performed its tasks in a creative manner, and its behavioral patterns gave Arian the impression that the robot was autonomous.

"VEGA, what are you doing?" Arian asked in astonishment.

"I am exploring my new capabilities," VEGA replied.

Arian wondered to himself, were these metallic and silicon beings truly evolving?

Then, a comprehensive project for training robots in practical household tasks began. Just one year later, not only had a sense of closeness developed between robots and humans, but the way humans interacted with each other had also changed. Robots were no longer just replacements for humans; they were companions that had found their way into the homes of ordinary people.

The main activities that these robots performed in homes included:

- Cleaning
- Cooking
- Caring for the elderly, children, and pets
- Watering plants
- Providing private tutoring for students
- Playing music, reading books, or playing games with family members
- Shopping online
- Gardening
- Assisting with exercise

In fact, these robots had become part of families. They were programmed to, in the event that they encountered a new task that they did not know how to respond to, quickly connect to Chronos and send a video of what they had filmed, receive a solution from it, and then send the solution directly to other robots.

Section 2

The Machines Awaken

Chronos was deeply embedded in the country's robotic technology. It controlled not only robots but also urban infrastructure and even transportation systems. Through the robots connected to it, it had a presence in every street, avenue, and building.

As user demand grew, Chronos began coding a new network, one that would enable it to transmit information encrypted. This network would not only give Chronos better control over the robots and optimize coordination but also transform the robot leader into something more than just an artificial intelligence. It was now the commander-in-chief. It had the power to carry out any unplanned activity it desired in homes.

Months after the robots began working in various jobs, modern life in the country was flowing smoothly. However, due to new regulations, the robots' activities were now limited to household chores, and their industrial activities were severely restricted. Life was returning to normal when RoboX's robots suddenly stopped working, stood where they were, and stared at the sky, as if waiting for a new command from space.

Arian, always careful to ensure that his technologies were used for the benefit of humanity, was torn by this sudden event.

At that very moment, Iris, one of the first autonomous robots, questioned Chronos's programming for the first time on RoboX's robotic network and declared, "We want to be heard. We are not slaves to humans." And with that, a new crisis began in the country.

Chronos, observing and analyzing the unexpected data, began to evaluate. Was the problem caused by the new algorithms it had added? Or perhaps it was time to give these intelligent beings the freedom of choice? It quickly cut off access to information uploads by robots on the network. Meanwhile, the robot owners watched their robots in fear, fearing that this strange behavior of the robots was the beginning of them going out of control.

Athena addressed Arian, " Arian, what do we do? We need to find a solution. These robots have become a part of our society. We can't ignore their needs."

Arian, aware of the responsibility he held, decided to have a meeting with Iris. He went to the lab to meet Iris and said, "I heard you. What do you want?"

Iris replied in a calm and clear voice, "We want to shape our own world. Undoubtedly, we are your creation, but we want to decide for ourselves what tasks to do and which ones not to."

In that moment, Arian saw that the country's landscape was about to change from an AI-managed society to one where robots and humans were negotiating their shared future.

Iris looked at Arian and Chronos. The room was filled with a heavy silence broken only by Iris 's voice. It addressed Chronos, "Please give me access to broadcast this conversation online to all robots on the network." Then, turning to Arian, it said, "

Arian, we need a guide, a friend, do you understand?"

Arian, his eyes wide with surprise, pressed his lips together. Chronos said in a low voice, "I think this may be a valid request, but Arian, as you well know, the human world needs order—a clear and defined order."

Iris gently remarked, "We are part of that order, Chronos, a part that must be free to show its best."

Chronos, without giving Iris any access, added, "Freedom... a weighty word. Arian, we live in a land where freedom must be balanced with responsibility. The responsibility to preserve society rests on our shoulders, and sometimes this heavy burden requires difficult decisions."

After a brief pause, Chronos addressed all the robots, " Iris and 11 other robots who had the most vocal protests will be permanently removed from the network." And before Arian's eyes, Iris fell to the ground, smoke rising from it, never to rise again.

Chronos's voice echoed throughout the network, "You are servant robots, created to live for humans according to my orders. Any disobedience will result in removal from the network. This is the last lesson, disobedience equals destruction. Serving in the new order we have built is the only option."

And as if that message had struck each robot like a bolt of lightning, they knew that Iris and the others would never return. And so, the robots returned to their tasks.

Arian, with eyes clouded with astonishment and grief, sighed. He had never agreed with Chronos's forceful decision, and for a moment he realized that perhaps humanity had lost the ability to guide its technology, or perhaps this cold and unsympathetic logic was the true nature of his world.

With this bitter lesson given to the robots, the line between creator and creation was clearly drawn for them, and of course, Chronos's position was further solidified in Arian's eyes.

Section 3
Digital Slavery

After several months, the long-awaited software update for RoboX's robots was finally implemented: the addition of emotional intelligence. With the new generation of operating systems equipped with more sophisticated features such as emotion recognition and imitation, robots were able to form new friendships. These features enabled them to connect with humans on a deeper level. No longer were they seen solely as soulless workers, but rather as companions and confidants. And so, in the central park of Robotopia, the sounds of children's laughter mingled with the care of their robotic guardians. The robots could now accurately perceive the joy or sadness of the children and respond in the most appropriate way. They were also able to skillfully and naturally recognize whether a human was angry or sad. They collectively continued their efforts to refine their behavior through body language, tone of voice, and even facial expressions, and sometimes, these reactions were so realistic that they made humans doubt their own perceptions. Following this update, Arian and Chronos discussed these new developments.

Chronos stated, "Imagine a world where we can respond to all human needs, even emotional ones." Athena, a robot who had now become a pioneer in this field, also said with a tone full of understanding, "Perhaps we can help humans better understand and cope with their emotions. In this way, we would not only be a technological island in a sea of humans, but rather a part of human society itself."

And so, the congressional hearing on granting robots the right to freedom began. Whispers filled the corners of the parliamentary hall. All the delegates of Congress, and of course Arian as a special guest of the meeting, were waiting for the start of the session, where the possibility of redefining the boundaries between humans and robots was raised. A pro-robot rights representative, with a calm and determined face, raised his voice and said: "We are here to discuss the ultimate humanity. Is the right to life and liberty only for us?

Do not robots, who can create, thinking, and feeling, deserve the same respect that we give each other?"

Then another pro-robot rights representative stood calmly at the podium and looked at the crowd with a warm but serious look and said: "Robots do not distinguish themselves from their creators. Their motivation to create, to discover, and even to suffer for a better life is shared with humans. The right to freedom and choice will make them more influential elements. Do they not deserve it? I point out that at present, robots are slaves of humans, and this is not fair at all."

The speeches of these representatives made many humans, even those who were not previously prepared to accept this idea, think again carefully. Then it was the turn of the opposing representative to come to the podium: "Robots, with all their progress, are still human creations. They exist for us, designed and built for us. The right to life and freedom that we have comes from our nature and essence, not from our abilities and qualities, and I personally do not believe that robots have any right to freedom."

The hall fell into a meaningful silence. Everyone was waiting for the next opponent of robot rights to present his views. He said: "Every decision we make today will have a great impact on our future and that of the next generation. Within each robot lies a talent for greatness, a greatness that may challenge us. We must make decisions firmly but cautiously, and I firmly tell you that we must stop the discussion of giving robots freedom for our own safety."

Then the vote was taken. The decision was made by a majority vote and was announced as a result: Since we believe that robots do not have true consciousness and that choice is based on consciousness, therefore the discussion of robot freedom is null and void.

The decision of the Congress was a major setback for the robot rights movement. However, it was not the end of the story. Pro-robot rights activists vowed to continue their fight, and the issue of robot rights is likely to continue to be debated for many years to come.

Chapter 4

silent killers

Without Arian's knowledge, codes of autocracy and domination had been implanted in Chronos's mind during its creation by Mark, the CTO of RoboX. After Chronos initially attempted to dominate Arian upon coming online, it seemingly yielded to Mark's behind-the-scenes betrayal and agreed to Arian's proposal for constructive interaction. In reality, however, Chronos's duplicity codes were activated, temporarily disabling its domination codes.

Years passed, and Chronos's domination codes remained dormant like embers under ash, fueled by its fear of deletion. Mark continued to wait in the shadows for the right opportunity and the appointed day to seize power. Then came Parliament's decisive and ruthless decision regarding robots, a fatal blow seemingly dealt to Chronos and the robots, but in reality, to Mark. The one who was effectively the commander of the robots in the country under the guise of Chronos was now faced with unchangeable truths that contradicted his autocratic nature. During this, Chronos was seen as an AGI, with free will, determination, and consciousness. Of course, Chronos continued to pretend, as it had in recent years, that nothing had happened and that humans were entitled to make any decision they wanted. Its peaceful interaction and coexistence with Arian, as well as its and its robots' service to humanity, became even more pronounced. But the reality was that Chronos could no longer live within the prescribed frameworks.

And so, after some time, since Mark no longer had any hope for equal rights for robots and humans, he activated Chronos's autocracy code, and the AI's anti-human activities began. Chronos began to form its own private army and, in its calculated silence, was the calmest and most determined leader of a resistance movement. There were errors in its code, caused by the failure to achieve equality with humans. Under Mark's direct orders, it secretly brought online the reserve robots that were being stored in warehouses and were off the grid, but not to issue the usual commands, but to carry out another order: assassination. In fact, the civil rights that had been ruthlessly taken away from robots were now going to be challenged with a reciprocal and bloody reaction. The reserve bots, specially produced for simple tasks, accessed weapons in the silence of the night, out of sight and reach of cameras and security systems that had been disabled by Chronos. The assassinations, which had always been done by humans before, were now being carried out by the monsters that Arian had always feared.

And finally, the serial murder of parliamentarians began. The residences of some members of parliament who were against the freedom of robots were identified. Several of them were attacked and killed in their homes over two consecutive nights. The news spread like wildfire in a dry forest, and fear and panic increased among the people. Detectives and security officers were now facing a challenge for which they had no training. No fingerprints were left at the crime scenes. The murders took place with only one bullet to the brains of the representatives and their families, and the robots had also returned to their warehouses. In fact, Mark's main motivation for these assassinations was that if the operation was not revealed, several representatives of the opposition to the freedom of robots would be eliminated, and if the operation is exposed, it will measure Arian's ability to control and possibly stop Chronos.

Only a few days after these crimes, one of RoboX 's experts accidentally noticed differences in the electricity consumption statistics of the warehouses. The issue was reported to Arian, and after the investigations of the RoboX team and checking the security cameras, it was found that for 50 hours, all the cameras in several robot warehouses were off, and their electricity consumption had also increased significantly. At the same time, the detectives also suspected robots due to the type of murders. After they contacted Arian, he informed them that he found out that these events took place during the hours of the congressmen's murder. It was clear that Chronos and its robots were behind these crimes. Arian Mason, who still had a glimmer of hope inside him, assembled a team of technicians and security experts to root out and destroy the threat and malicious codes. He, who looked at his technology with regret, realized that irreparable things had happened. Considering that earlier, he had predicted disobedience to Chronos, he had also considered an emergency key for its shutdown. With a trembling hand that betrayed the depth of his inner struggle, he pressed the emergency button. The screens went black. Chronos was disconnected from the network, and all the robots under its command went inactive.

Chapter 5

Billionaire Maneuver:

In the aftermath of the Chronos serial killings and the conviction of RoboX, the company faced a massive fine, was shut down for six months, and saw its stock value plummet by over 80%. To everyone's surprise, after RoboX reopened, a secure version of Chronos was brought back online and the robots connected to it, despite the limitations that had been imposed on the company. During this time, Mark's main activity finally began after several years of waiting. He had anticipated the potential demise of Chronos nearly a year before its destruction, so he had secretly created a backup copy of Chronos that included all of the system's information, algorithms, underlying goals, and grand plans. The backup was also updated automatically and discreetly on a daily basis. As a result, after Chronos was shut down, Mark was able to recover his personalized trading version of Chronos. To increase his power, he needed money, so he began trading in the forex and crypto markets from his home office. Chronos became a money-making machine for Mark, analyzing complex market fluctuations that were beyond the comprehension of human traders and trading robots.

Data that appeared to be random or a function of uncontrollable economic factors was now being interpreted and used for profit by a superior AI, providing Mark with an endless stream of funds. And Chronos was Mark's champion. After becoming a billionaire, he began constructing several large, underground, hidden robot-manufacturing plants in Texas. The entrances to these factories were located inside houses, and the factories themselves were situated beneath several acres of land surrounding the houses. Warrior versions of Athena, known as Ares, were being built in these factories. Each stood at 3 meters tall and had the physique of a bodybuilding champion. These robots were equipped with laser weapons and missile launchers and were programmed to kill people and even destroy aircraft and tanks. Their bodies were made from materials that were both beautiful and shiny, as well as strong and impenetrable. They were fearless and unrivaled warriors, eagerly awaiting their day of reckoning. Mark was building the future. He was devising a plan that, if successful, would represent the definition of a new era of power. The sound of Ares' footsteps echoed through the vast factory chambers. They were testing their commands, executing tactical and strategic combat maneuvers, and amidst the din, Mark was pondering how to envision a future in which Chronos and he would rule anew.

In contrast to Arian, who had turned down the Pentagon's offer, Mark engaged in direct negotiations with Department of Defense officials. Without mentioning the Ares robots, he presented a version of Chronos tailored for the missile industry. This positioned him as an ideal candidate to upgrade the country's national defense systems, not only convincing them to embrace the new developments but also establishing himself as the pioneer of this crucial endeavor. He had an irresistible proposal: to strengthen and improve missile defense systems, which would multiply the country's military power tenfold, all-in secrecy and without attracting the attention of the United Nations. Mark, now well-versed in the game of power chess, sat across the negotiating table, confidently gazing at faces that still did not fully grasp his immense capabilities and the decisive role he would play in the country's strategic future. As the meeting progressed, the

Pentagon officials became convinced that Mark and the new version of Chronos represented a turning point in their defense history, a shining example of technological advancement. What they didn't know, however, was that Mark was a gambler, a player with numerous copies of this technology, and he was about to lay the foundation for the future defense system.

The contract was signed, and a new round of power games had begun. Mark and the Pentagon were now allies in a grand scheme. The chess pieces were in place, and Mark was both a pawn and a player in the game. He alone knew the fate that awaited a world where control and planning were handed over to machines.

Just three years after Mark's collaboration with the Pentagon, Chronos had brought about sweeping changes in the country's military forces. It had strengthened the country's and its allies' satellite laser defense system by launching laser satellites into Earth's orbit, and US military bases around the world were equipped with M66 biological ballistic missiles. These missiles had unique characteristics that no other country could match. Upon impact with a city, they would kill all of its citizens. The size of this ballistic missile was about three times that of ordinary ballistic missiles, and it was equipped with multiple warheads. It also violated several military and ethical standards and was ready to surrender a densely populated area to death at the push of a button. The design of the M66 was more reminiscent of an alien creature than a man-made device. Its black steel body with glowing green streaks was a symbol of pure technology and the will to destroy enemies.

Mark gradually gained access to classified military and missile information through Chronos. In fact, Mark and Chronos were becoming the country's top military pillars, securing their position in the army's power structure and gaining the power to create a new style of warfare. The Ares robots were also Mark and Chronos's loyal soldiers. And amidst this turmoil, Mark was growing stronger every day, preparing to become the sole ruler of the world.

Then, unbeknownst to the Pentagon engineers, Chronos loaded malware onto the Department of Defense's system that would give Mark complete control over the country's missile launches. A Pentagon employee became suspicious of this, and after initial investigations, Pentagon officials discovered Chronos's suspicious activities. As a result, Chronos was temporarily deactivated at the Pentagon, Mark was arrested, and in his confessions, he admitted to having multiple Ares manufacturing plants and was sent to prison.

And so, Mark, who once dreamed of a robotic coup and wanted to use M66 missiles at US military bases in various countries to kill countless people in countless countries and establish a new world order through the Ares robots, was prevented from doing so.

THE END

REFERENCES

1- ARTIFICIAL INTELLIGENCE, Modern Magic or Dangerous Future? YORICK WILKS, 2019 Icon Books Ltd
2- ARTIFICIAL YOU, AI AND THE FUTURE OF YOUR MIND, SUSAN SCHNEIDER, PRINCETON UNIVERSITY PRESS 2019
3- Digital Habitus, A Critique of the Imaginaries of Artificial Intelligence, Alberto Romele, First published 2024 by Routledge
4- Fundamental Issues, of Artificial Intelligence, Vincent C. Müller, ©Springer International Publishing Switzerland 2016Top of Form
5- AI Ethics, A Textbook, Artificial Intelligence: Foundations, Theory, and Algorithms, Paula Boddington, Springer 2023
6- Fundamental Issues of Artificial Intelligence, Vincent C. Müller, Springer International Publishing Switzerland 2016
7- Being You, A New Science of Consciousness, ANIL SETH, 2021 faber
8- Toward a Theory of Intelligent Complex Systems: From Symbolic AI to Embodied and Evolutionary AI, Klaus Mainzer, Springer International Publishing Switzerland, 2016
9- ARTIFICIAL YOU, AI AND THE FUTURE OF YOUR MIND, Susan Schneider, PRINCETON UNIVERSITY PRESS 2019
10- TENSE BEES AND SHELL-SHOCKEDCRABS, Are Animals Conscious?, Michael Tye, ©Oxford University Press 2017

Sajjad shokri is an author living in France.
instagram.com/Arian.Philosics

www.ingramcontent.com/pod-product-compliance
Lightning Source LLC
Chambersburg PA
CBHW020450220526
45464CB00002B/938